Contents

Look out for the jealousy monster!

Look out for the jealousy monster!

He's sneaky and he's strange,

And the moment that you meet him

Your mood will start to change.

He'll make you feel gloomy and grumpy,

He'll make you feel sulky and sad,

That grumbling, green-eyed monster,

Look out for him – he's **BAD**!

4

Keep out of my way!

Keep out of my way!

Keep out of my way!

I'm jealous of **EVERYONE** today.

If I were a dog

I'd be jealous of a cat.

If I were a mouse

I'd be jealous of a rat.

If I were a circle

I'd be jealous of a square.

If I were an apple

I'd be jealous of a pear.

I know I'm silly

To feel this way.

But I'm jealous of **EVERYONE** today.

5

What about me?

What about me?

What about me?

I'm sitting here scowling,

Can't anyone see?

You've nagged at my brother

Since quarter past three,

But **NOBODY'S** bothered

To grumble at **ME**!

Scribble scream

I drew a happy,

Sunny day,

Scribbled on it

Straight away.

Jealous lines

Of swirly steam.

What's it called?

A Scribble Scream!

Who cares?

So what if the baby's walking?

What if it gurgles? Who cares?

I can bounce on the sofa,

I can slide down the stairs,

I can climb up the curtains,

I can frighten the cat,

I can roar like a tiger . . .

Does **ANYONE** notice that?

8

It's Mum and Dad who are naughty,

I'm sure you must have guessed.

It's **THEIR** fault I've broken my teddy,

It's **THEIR** fault I'm being a pest,

And it serves them right,

It serves them right,

For loving the baby best.

Don't blame me

9

The best bike

The boy next door
Has bought a bike –
The sort of bike
I'd **REALLY** like.

But as **MY** bike's
A perfect fit,
I'll try to make
The best of it.

Good loser

When my brother
Wins our games
I want to call him
Nasty names.

If instead

I don't give in –

Some day soon

I'm **SURE** to win.

Brother bother

I hate it when my brother
Has a special treat.

I'm jealous of the fun he'll have
In Gran and Grandad's street.

I love it when my cousin
Comes to stay all night –
And I bet my brother's jealous
Of our sleepy pillow fight!

15

Pencil power

I was jealous this morning,

What could I do?

I picked up my pencils,

I drew and I drew.

My house in the sunshine,

My teddy and Spot,

My Mum and my Dad . . .

And who's jealous?

I'm not!

Whenever I feel jealous,

(Which happens now and then)

I think of fun days

In the sun days,

And soon I smile again.

Sunny smiles

The best cure

The **BEST** cure I've found

For jealousy

Is knowing the others

Are jealous of **ME**.

Three cheers

Michael and his sister Sophie,

How they hate my swimming trophy,

How they frown at me today

When the others shout, "**HOORAY**!"

Everyone's jealous

Everyone's jealous of someone
Whether they like it or not.
My best friend wants my skateboard
(A thing he hasn't got.)

And yesterday I even wished
I had four paws, like Spot!!

The magic trick

Here's a little magic trick,
It's simple and it's neat
Jealousy will vanish if
You give your friend a treat.

If people were like teddies

No one would be jealous
If people were like bears,
My teddy **NEVER** changes,
My teddy **ALWAYS** cares.

When Mum and Dad are busy,
Or when it's not my day,
When all my friends are mean to me
My teddy's here to stay.

If people were like teddies,
If friends could be like bears,
NO ONE would be jealous –
A teddy **ALWAYS** cares.

22